And the *Beat* Goes On

KEEPING YOUR LIFE, YOUR TIME, AND YOUR SOUL IN DIVINE RHYTHM

EQUATOR STROMAN CHEEK

WESTBOW
PRESS®
A DIVISION OF THOMAS NELSON
& ZONDERVAN

Scripture taken from the King James Version of the Bible.

Scripture taken from the New King James Version®. Copyright © 1982 by Thomas Nelson. Used by permission. All rights reserved.

Scripture quotations marked (NIV) are taken from the Holy Bible, New International Version®, NIV®. Copyright © 1973, 1978, 1984, 2011 by Biblica, Inc.™ Used by permission of Zondervan. All rights reserved worldwide. www.zondervan.com The "NIV" and "New International Version" are trademarks registered in the United States Patent and Trademark Office by Biblica, Inc.™

Scripture quotations are taken from the Holy Bible, New Living Translation, copyright ©1996, 2004, 2007, 2013, 2015 by Tyndale House Foundation. Used by permission of Tyndale House Publishers, Inc., Carol Stream, Illinois 60188. All rights reserved.

Scripture quotations marked MSG are taken from THE MESSAGE, copyright © 1993, 1994, 1995, 1996, 2000, 2001, 2002 by Eugene H. Peterson. Used by permission of NavPress. All rights reserved. Represented by Tyndale House Publishers, Inc.

This book is a work of non-fiction. Unless otherwise noted, the author and the publisher make no explicit guarantees as to the accuracy of the information contained in this book and in some cases, names of people and places have been altered to protect their privacy.

WestBow Press books may be ordered through booksellers or by contacting:

WestBow Press
A Division of Thomas Nelson & Zondervan
1663 Liberty Drive
Bloomington, IN 47403
www.westbowpress.com
1 (866) 928-1240

Because of the dynamic nature of the Internet, any web addresses or links contained in this book may have changed since publication and may no longer be valid. The views expressed in this work are solely those of the author and do not necessarily reflect the views of the publisher, and the publisher hereby disclaims any responsibility for them.

Any people depicted in stock imagery provided by Thinkstock are models, and such images are being used for illustrative purposes only.
Certain stock imagery © Thinkstock.

ISBN: 978-1-5127-9365-9 (sc)
ISBN: 978-1-5127-9366-6 (e)

Library of Congress Control Number: 2017910919

Print information available on the last page.

WestBow Press rev. date: 08/15/2017

In loving memory of Carrie Mae Wright, my mother

CONTENTS

Carrie Mae Wright, also known as "NaNa" to her grandchildren, was in a league all her own. The second youngest of ten siblings, she was born and raised in South Carolina. When she was old enough, she made her way to Washington, DC. She mastered the trade of a seamstress, and her home cooking was one to die for.

One thing about Carrie was that she loved her children and grandchildren and she would do anything for them. Even today, though sometimes it seems so hard to cope with the thought of Mama not being here, I must stop and remember she's not gone. She just went to meet me at the place where one day I will see her again.

I remember her neatness, her beauty, and her smile. I recall the time she spent in the kitchen baking those cakes and them sweet potato pies. I think of her sewing machine and the things she stitched—the countless quilts, blankets, and many clothes. I remember the early hours of the morning she worked perfecting her garden, raking, digging, watering, and planting those fruits, veggies, and good-smelling flowers.

There is one last thing I must not forget but always remember, the morals and values she taught me as a child. Those things with God first in my life have brought me this far not to leave me now. And though Mama has gone on home, the memories of her still live strong. For you see, I am a part of her, and part of her lives in me.

INTRODUCTION

INTRODUCTION

This book is being written with the inspiration of the Holy Spirit. The noun *spirit* relates to a verb meaning "to breathe." The spirit of life is God's gift to all creatures (Job 12:10; Ecclesiastes 12:7 NKJV). The endowment of God's Holy Spirit is a gift to believers, bringing spiritual life (Psalm 143:10 NKJV), power (Judges 6:34 NKJV), wisdom, understanding (Isaiah 11:2 NKJV), and divine revelation, leading to an understanding of God's Word and His perfect ways (Joel 2:28 NKJV). *Inspired* in Hebrew is *theopneustos*, which means "the very breath of God." As you read from the pages of this book, know that they encompass the inspired Word of God.

Story

I remember being in church and my pastor having a special prayer service. Sitting beside me was a young lady who turned to me and said, "Here we are having special prayer, and my husband is sitting over there upset with me."

I turned to her and said these words, "And the beat goes on."

Then I reached out and held her hand as Pastor began to pray. Amazingly enough, our paths never crossed again until several months later. I had just arrived at church when this young lady spoke to me and smiled. I didn't quite know who she was when she spoke. I thought she was just being friendly, but after the service, I saw her again as I was walking to my car.

She stopped and said to me, "I will never forget what you said to me several months ago."

As she spoke, I thought to myself, Clearly, she has me mixed up with someone else.

Nevertheless, I listened as she told me how my words had meant so much in her life. Even then, I still believed this was a case of mistaken identity, but I listened anyway as she started to recall the night we had sat together.

She said that later that evening, after she had spoken and prayed with me, when she and her husband returned home, he brought up the same thing he had been upset about before going to the service.

As he spoke, she simply looked him straight in the face and said, "And the beat goes on."

He looked at her like she was crazy, and she just walked away. It wasn't until she uttered those five short words that I realized she was in fact referring to the encounter with me. As we parted ways that night, the Holy Spirit spoke to me about the specific areas of influence and motivation God has given to me by His grace. It was clear that the Holy Spirit wanted to use this saying to have a unique impact on the lives of others, just as it has greatly influenced my life over the years I've been saying those words and living by them.

***

I am not exactly sure what made me start saying the five words "and the beat goes on." But for many years now, it has been a life principle that gives me divine peace in my heart and mind when I am faced with situations and circumstances that tempt me to worry or remain in the emotional strongholds of hurt and disappointment.

When I say, "And the beat goes on," it reminds me of a commonly used English language adage, "This too shall pass." Unfortunately, people often use this phrase when working through difficult circumstances in life and give credit to the Bible; however, those exact words are not found there. But what is found is "And it shall come to pass" (Genesis 24:43, 27:40, 47:24; Deuteronomy 28:1 NKJV, just to name a few spots where you can find this phrase).

The strongest word in that saying is *shall*, which means "will happen in the future" or "intended to happen." What I am saying is that God is going to bring to pass what He has promised. This is good news for you and me. God understands the situation more than you think. God has promised that every evil counsel against you cannot stand. It shall come to pass. He has promised that good and mighty things will happen in your life. He shall bring it to pass. He promised that you will eat the good of the land. He shall bring it to pass. He says all the enemies confronting you shall be defeated. He shall bring it to pass. He promised that you and your children will be for signs and wonders. He shall bring it to pass. He promised deliverance from all your troubles. It shall come to pass. Any force or power hindering what God has promised in your life will wither in the name of Jesus. Remember this scripture in 2 Peter 3:9 (NKJV), "The Lord is not slack concerning His promise, as some count slackness, but is longsuffering toward us, not willing that any should perish but that all should come to repentance."

Psalm 107:26–29 (NKJV) tells us,

> They mount up to the heaven. They go down again to the depths: their soul is melted because of trouble. They reel to and fro, and stagger like a drunken man, and are at their wit's end. Then they cry unto the Lord in their trouble, and He brings them out of their distresses. He calms the storm, so that its waves are still.

People looking for help have tried everything they know—Mama, Daddy, friends, preachers, teachers, and even psychologists. And nothing is working. They are confused, and then—and only then—do they cry unto the Lord God Almighty. God will calm the troubled seas and perform His Word. Jeremiah 1:12 (NLT) states, "And the LORD said, that's right, and it means that I am watching, and I will certainly carry out all my plans."

There are some things you must do if you want the promises of God for your life to come to pass. It is important because, despite His promises, a believer may face some tests and troubles, especially while waiting for the fulfillment of these promises. Remember this: His love has no limit, His grace has no measure, and His power has no boundary known unto men.

The following is what a Christian should not engage in because these can cause delays in the arrival of God's promises:

- Do not blame God! (There is no fault in Him.)
- Do not break down!
- Do not give up!
- Do not be discouraged!
- Do not lose your joy!
- Do not give in to worrying!
- Do not fear!

When you engage in these things, it is a sign that you do not believe that God can make a way. The power of God takes off when human power ends or fails. Instead a believer should do the following to hasten the fulfillment of the promises of God to make sure he or she inherits all that God has set aside for him or her:

- Rejoice in the Lord always. Again, I say "Rejoice!"
- Seek to know from God what is going on. (Most times, a delay is for your own good because it will clear the way so you can enjoy your blessings to the fullest level. Instead of crying and brooding over a situation, go to the Lord in prayer and let Him reveal His will to you.)
- Determine to view the crisis as an opportunity.
- Refuse unscriptural advice.
- Persevere.
- Live a holy life.
- Commit your ways unto the Lord.
- Trust and obey God. (Lean not to your own understanding, but in all your ways, acknowledge Him and leave all the consequences to Him.)

He shall bring it to pass. God does not need your manipulation or engineering to fulfill His purpose in your life. When you do these things, that great promise, "It shall come to pass," will surely happen in your life. Many people have been breaking the laws of faith and are expecting wonderful things to happen. What they are inviting is defeat.

Now when I think about the words "and the beat goes on," the first thing that comes to my mind is the heart. In life and in our natural state, the heart must continue to beat in the right rhythm, if we are to remain in the land of the living. Along with that, I also think about a heart monitor screen of an echocardiogram that doctors use. If there is a beat, there is life. No matter what goes on through the day or how many altercations you may have, the beat of the heart continues. Yes, it may change pace, but it will continue to beat. You may lie down or sit as still as possible, but your heartbeat continues. This is how we should view challenging situations in our lives. No matter what, we must learn to exercise that measure of faith (Romans 12:3 NKJV) that God has given to us, look at those challenges, and say, "And this too shall pass."

We must learn to be optimist, not pessimistic, about those things in our lives—be it a toxic relationship, financial difficulty, or health problem. Always concentrate on the positive and not the negative. It's like the adage, except the things you cannot change then change the things you can. Ask God to give you the wisdom to know the difference. We must take that God-given wisdom and use it. I am reminded of two scriptures. Isaiah 26:3 (KJV) says, "Thou wilt keep him in perfect peace, whose mind is stayed on thee, because he trusteth in thee." And Romans 8:6 (KJV) states, "For to be carnally minded is death; but to be spiritually minded is life and peace."

When you stop worrying but instead pray with thanksgiving in every situation, knowing that your life, your time, and your soul has already moved on, it is then and only then that you will experience God's peace as your guardian. Romans 8:28 (NKJV) tells us, "And we know that all things work together for good to those who love God, to those who are the called according to His purpose."

1

THE RHYTHM OF LIFE: SOME RAIN MUST FALL

1

THE RHYTHM OF LIFE: SOME RAIN MUST FALL

Story

The songwriter puts it just the way I want to begin this story. "Up drove the hearse Cadillac. A crowd of people gathered round it all dressed in black, and as they removed the body from the car, such pain I never knew did fill my heart."

Yes, that body was my brother Greg, and my mind began to remember the cause of this event. It was late in the evening, and my husband and I were relaxing and watching television in the bedroom when suddenly the phone rang. My husband answered to the sound of the person on the other end screaming. He then proceeded to hand me the phone, stating that it sounded like my niece Shaleya.

I grabbed the phone and immediately told Shaleya to calm down and tell me what was going on. In that moment, everything became surreal. She kept screaming, "He's dead! He's dead!"

Uncertain of what could possibly be going on, I asked the question, "Who's dead?"

And that was when she said, "Dad."

In a state of disbelief, I inquired further, "What do mean Dad?"

Through tears, she relayed that her dad, my brother, was cutting down some trees in the backyard and one must have fallen on him, trapping him. And he died.

The realization that my brother, my friend, was gone brought that pain I never knew could fill my heart. I had just talked to my brother on the phone earlier that week, so hearing that he was dead felt so wrong.

I asked, "Lord, what have I done to deserve this misery?" And I began to ask myself if life would ever be the same again.

This wasn't the first death I had experienced of someone close to me, but when our loved ones die unexpectedly, that loss is often harder to cope with. As Christians, we know, at death, the soul of believers enters the presence of the Lord (2 Corinthians 5:8 NKJV). We just don't have control over God's clock. I had to accept the fact that my brother had gone on to a better place not made by hands. He can't come back to me, but one day I will go to where he is.

So, I end this story the same way I started, with the lyrics of a song by Marvin Winans,

"I Won't Complain"

I've had some good days,
I've had some hills to climb,
I've had some weary days,
I've had some sleepless nights,
But when I look around And I think things over,
All of my good days Outweigh my bad days.

***

James 4:14 (NKJV) reminds us, "Whereas you do not know what *will happen* tomorrow. For what *is* your life? It is even a vapor that appears for a little time and then vanishes away." Sometimes we don't even understand how little control we have over life itself. It seems like some rain must fall in every situation of life—rain of pain, rain of disappointments, rain of defeats, rain of tears, and rain of fears. But life must and will go on!

Do you remember your rainy season when it seemed like nothing you said or did went right, the weight was great, and the valley you were in was deeper than ever? You were in a rain of despair. You've been telling God every day about the things you're going through. They have you worried and discouraged and feeling badly too. The burdens are just too heavy for you to bear. But though you cry out to the Lord, it seems as if He doesn't hear you, so you cry a little louder, for it's all too much to take. You hope God will finally hear you and help you, for goodness's sake. Always remember: delay doesn't mean denial.

But just when you've convinced yourself God has turned away His ear, the Lord will begin to speak to you, and He will calmly say, "My child, I know you're hurting, and I see that you're upset. But don't let the things you're going through cause you to forget that I never break a promise."

Jeremiah 29:11–13 (NKJV) reminds me,

> For I know the thoughts that I think toward you, says the Lord, thoughts of peace and not of evil, to give you a future and a hope. Then you will call upon Me and go and pray to Me, and I will listen to you. And you will seek Me and find *Me,* when you search for Me with all your heart.

God knows it's hard to understand all the things He must take you through, but you must trust Him and believe He is working it out for your good. Don't depend on yourself, for in Him is your strength to cope. Things in life aren't always good, and though your trials, they may increase. He'll work each situation until a blessing is released. Not just some but all. Not even this or that. He said, "all things" and meant it. And that's where the truth is at.

God never breaks a promise, and because of what He said, He'll take those things you're going through and work them for your good. He tells you to be encouraged and calls you His friend (John 15:13–15 NKJV). Remember, God is always with us in the now, that moment we need Him. Thank God for being ever-present. He is always there, always listening, and always ready to help us. God will work it out!

If it is healing you need, you must realize healing comes about through a change of consciousness or heart through forgiveness of others, yourself, life, and God. Isaiah 53:5 (NKJV) tells us, "But He *was* wounded for our transgressions, He was bruised for our iniquities; The chastisement for our peace *was* upon Him, And by His stripes we are healed."

1 Peter 2:24 (NKJV) tells us, "Who Himself bore our sins in His own body on the tree, that we, having died to sins, might live for righteousness—by whose stripes you were healed." Healing comes when you relinquish your beliefs about what the conditions of your life should have been and become willing to accept and eventually even appreciate what simply is.

As you continue to move forward on this life's journey, you may know how and when to expect, but accepting is another issue all by itself. You must learn to accept.

Acceptance is a virtue whose value often goes unremarked, yet what a powerful virtue it is. Acceptance is a choice you can make. And once you choose to accept things as they are, you become more open, your pain and anger dissipate, and everyone around you feels the calm you feel.

Acceptance is not resignation. Resignation implies defeat. Acceptance is our willingness to let them be and learn to wait on the Lord. You must stop and think about how many times God has already broken your chains and set you free. It is amazing how He always seem to come right in the nick of time. When you think all hope is gone or God has forgotten all about you, here He comes sometimes in the morning, occasionally in the noonday, or from time to time late at night. He will come in your room, giving you just a touch, a reminder that everything will be all right. He reminds you that weeping may endure for a night, but joy comes in the morning (Psalm 30:5 NKJV).

Remember, prayer and faith is the key, but also recall that praying does not guarantee you will get everything you request. God follows no single pattern in responding to His children's requests. Sometimes you can go through your whole life being denied the very desire of your heart because He knows what is best for his begging child. When you pray to God for help, it is a request, not a demand for action. God evaluates every prayer by His infinite wisdom and unfailing love. He gives only what He knows is best. It is a hurting thing to see something you want but cannot have: a man or woman you just knew was going to be your husband or wife, that car you saw in the showroom window, that baby you just cannot seem to have, or that house you have been dreaming about.

Wanting

Wanting not to want
Wanting to believe
Wanting to be loved
Wanting to be wanted for what's inside of me
Wanting not to fear
Wanting to trust
Wanting to be content in all I do
Wanting to be believed
Wanting not to hold back my feelings
Wanting to be all I should be
Wanting to be totally me!
R.A.S.

We go to God with ready-made plans for Him to bless and approve. Don't forget all things work together for the good to those who love God and are called according to His purpose (Romans 8:28–29 NKJV). And remember, you are always being prepared for something or protected from something worse.

When the divine reason for the meantime union has been fulfilled or the divine season for the meantime experience comes to an end, you will move exactly where you need to be. If you learn to hold out and hold on to the Word of God, who left on record that He will never leave you nor forsake you (Joshua 1:5 NIV), that pain will turn into gain. Those disappointments will turn into hope and desires. Those defeats will turn into victories. Those tears will turn into joy. And those fears, well, God did not give you the spirit of fear. Instead He gave you the spirit of power, love, and sound mind (2 Timothy 1:7 NKJV).

Just wait. God will rain down blessings. He wants to give you a great abundance of peace, love, and happiness. Remember, no part of life is outside His control. Though we can't see the outcome of life, we must trust the Lord because He knows what is best. Know this! God's desire is for us to be anchored in only Himself. Your day may seem bleak and dreary without a visibly ray of hope, yet He is present. Although we do not see God, Peter reminds us that we can love Him and rejoice in His love for us with "inexpressible," glorious joy (1 Peter 1:8 NKJV).

Amid all the clamor and dim of this visible and audible world, listen carefully for God's quiet voice. Listen to Him in the Bible, and talk to Him frequently in prayer. God tells you to hold out. A change will come, but in the meantime, life goes on! He left on record in His Word (Hosea 10:12 NKJV), "Sow for yourselves righteousness; reap in mercy; break up your fallow ground; for it is time to seek the Lord, till He comes and rains righteousness on you."

Your heart must be rooted and grounded in the Word so that what He says is final with you. Stop depending on your own strength. In all areas of your walk as a believer, you are incapable in your own strength and insufficient in your own resources to overcome the wiles and temptations of the devil. Let God take you to the next level, and you should begin to thank Him over and over again for what He is about to do in your life. The songwriter put it this way, "What God has for you it is for you." Yes, some rain must fall, but the rhythm of life will and must go on.

2
THE RHYTHM OF LIFE: PREPARE FOR THE CURVEBALL

2

THE RHYTHM OF LIFE: PREPARE FOR THE CURVEBALL

Story

It's Wednesday morning, and as I awaken, I thank God for another day and start my usual daily devotional exercise. I read my Daily Bread, and the title for that day is "Time for a Change."

After I read that, I turn on the television and do a twenty-minute workout. You see, I had been exercising, but only in my mind. This day I physically do it! Feeling good mentally and physically, I arrive at work. As I turn on my computer, I have a reminder to go have my cholesterol checked because the office is offering free tests. (By the way, my results were very good.)

I finish that and return to the office. After about an hour later, my program manager asks me to come in his office, and as I enter, there sits my manager. And I immediately say to myself, Lord, have mercy on me.

The program manager says, "I have bad news."

He tells me that they are having a reduction in force (RIF) and I am being let go, effective two weeks from that day. It is amazing after he uttered those words. I don't believe I hear anything else in that moment, even though my manager's lips are moving. My ears go completely silent. My mind takes me back in time, and I begin to think about what had occurred over the last couple months.

I had known something was up because the atmosphere around the office was different. My office mates had already been demoted from exempt to non-exempt, but up to now, because I had seniority, my status did not change. But little did I know they were plotting my demise. You talk about a "curveball" I was thrown. I didn't have a glove on to catch it, but God's mercy sustained me.

As time progressed, the Holy Spirit took me to a scripture in Micah 7:8 (NIV), "Do not gloat over me my enemy! Though I have fallen, I will rise."

And rise I did. I am happy to report that the Lord God Almighty did in fact bless me with a great job in the government, and let me also say I did not lose one dime salary wise. Thank you, Jesus.

***

As your life continues in this earthly vessel, sometimes the rhythm of life will throw you a curveball. The word "curve" means to deviate from the straight line, and the word "deviate" means to turn away from. God doesn't mind upsetting our plans if it produces character in us (Psalm 119:65–67 AMP).

On this life's journey, some of those curveballs will shake your very foundation. But God just says, "Count it all joy" (James 1:2 NKJV), reminding you again that He will not put no more on you than you can bear as long as you keep your mind stayed on Him, according to His wisdom and purpose, and keep our responsibility to trust and obey. So if you got it, that means you can handle it (1 Corinthians 10:13; Psalm 55:22, 68:19; Matthew 11:28; 1 Peter 5: 6–7).

Sometimes those words are easier said than done. I believe without a shadow of a doubt that God will take care of you. But sometimes the evil one comes with his curve of tricks, curve of deceptions, curve of temptations, and curve of false hopes that can catch you off guard and off God. But God is faithful! He has put enough in you when you accepted His Son to be able to take those curveballs and make them straight and keep on in Jesus's name, but you must be sold out to Jesus, meaning totally committed to Him. There is not one curveball Satan can throw that faith in God's Word cannot overcome.

You say it is an impossible curveball. God says, "The things which are impossible with men are possible with God" (Luke 18:2 NKJV).

You say you have a curveball of tiredness. God says, "Come to me, all you who labor and are heavy laden, and I will give you rest" (Matthew 11:28–30 NKJV).

You say you have a curveball of "nobody really loves me." God says, "I have loved you" (John 13:3 NKJV).

You say you have a curveball of "I can't go on." God says, "My grace is sufficient" (2 Corinthians 12:9 NKJV).

You say you have a "I can't figure things out" curveball. God says, "He shall direct your path" (Proverbs 3:5–6 NKJV).

You say you have a "I can't do it" curveball. God says, "You can do all things through Christ" (Philippians 4:13 NKJV).

You say you have a curveball of "I'm not able." God says, "He is able" (2 Corinthians 9:8 NKJV).

You say you have a curveball of "I can't forgive myself." God says, "He is faithful and just to forgive" (1 John 1:9 NKJV).

You say you have a curveball of "It's not worth it." God says, "All things work together for the good" (Romans 8:28 NKJV).

You say you have a curveball of "I can't manage." God says, "He will supply all your needs" (Philippians 4:19 NKJV).

You say you have a curveball of fear. God says, "He has not given you a spirit of fear" (2 Timothy 1:7 NKJV).

You say you have a curveball of "I'm always worried and frustrated." God says, "Cast all your cares upon Him" (1 Peter 5:7 NKJV).

You say you have a curveball of "I'm not smart enough." God says, "The Lord gives wisdom" (Proverbs 2:6 NKJV).

You say you have a curveball of "not enough faith." God says, "He has dealt to each one a measure of faith" (Romans 12:3 NKJV).

You must remember that, if you have five physical senses and a workable mind, you will be in contact with Satan. The

Bible tells us repeatedly that he is already defeated. James 4:7–8 (NKJV) states, "Therefore submit to God, resist the devil and he will flee from you. Draw near to God and He will draw near to you." Make sure during your curveball seasons that you don't turn away from the only help you know. The Bible tells us in Matthew 28:20 (NKJV), "And lo, I am with you always, even until the end of the age." It also tells us in Hebrews 13:5 (NKJV), "He will never leave you nor forsake you."

The key is faith. God's Word tells us that faith comes by hearing and hearing by the Word of God (Romans 10:17). The Bible also tells us that faith is the substance of things hoped for and the evidence of things not seen (Hebrews 11:1) and that we walk by faith, not by sight (2 Corinthians 5:7). Author E. W. Kenyon, who wrote *Advance Bible Course*, mentioned there are two kinds of faith:

1. Sense knowledge faith: This is the greatest enemy of faith because it demands physical evidence to satisfy the senses. For instance, before a person can see that he or she is healed or that he or she has the thing for which he or she prayed for, he or she must be able to touch, smell, taste, see, and hear it before accepting. We must learn to believe beyond what our senses register.

2. Word knowledge faith: This requires no evidence of the senses. It is spiritual knowledge. It is knowledge that has come to us through the re-created spirit by acting on the Word and living in it. It depends solely on the Word of God. He finds a passage of scripture that covers his need, and he makes that his

own. In our daily walk, the Holy Spirit is building into us a fearless confidence in the Word. We require no physical evidence to prove we are healed. When the Word of God says "Surely, He hath borne our sicknesses and carried our diseases that settle it for us," we are governed by the Word and not the five senses.

Author Reverend Harold Trammell, who wrote *Church Alive*, states,

Faith is a combination of three words: belief, acceptance, and trust. Grouped together, these words create the definition of faith. When one becomes a Christian, he must believe in Jesus Christ; he must accept Jesus Christ as his personal Savior; and he must trust Jesus Christ alone. This belief, acceptance, and trust forms the foundation of the Christian's confidence in Jesus and in His power to fulfill God's promise of salvation. In its simplest form, faith means loyalty.

Yes, faith is certainly an essential element in the Christian life.

a. "But without faith it is impossible to please Him, for he who comes to God must believe that He is, and that He is a rewarder of those who diligently seek Him" (Hebrews 11:6 NKJV).
b. "For by grace you have been saved through faith, and that not of yourselves; it is the gift of God" (Ephesians 2:8 NKJV).
c. "For we walk by faith, not by sight" (2 Corinthians 5:7 NKJV).

Remember, faith is a spiritual force that releases the ability of the power of God in you and through you. Faith is the Word of God. Again, the person who walks by faith in the Word of God requires no evidence of the senses. They have proof that the thing they are praying for has come. As long as you have your five senses and a workable mind, the enemy will always be on your trail. Make sure you are prayed up and tangled up in the Word of God. Prayer based upon the Word rises above the senses and contacts the author of the Word.

Christ has done everything necessary for us to endure in our faith. He is our example and model. His attention was not on the agonies of the cross, but on the crown. His attention was not on the suffering, but the reward. God tells us in the Gospel of John, "If you abide in me and my Word abides in you, you shall ask what you will, and it shall be done for you or brought into being." He also says in the book of Jeremiah, "I watch over my Word to perform it." Like a compass, the Bible always points you in the right direction.

Remember, how a person lives his or her life is a function of how he or she thinks. If a person's mind constantly feasts on earthly, everyday things, that person's source of strength and encouragement will be limited to the resources of the natural world. The Bible tells us in 2 Corinthians 10:5 (NKJV), "Casting down arguments and every high thing that exalts itself against the knowledge of God, bringing every thought into captivity to the obedience of Christ."

You can literally make sense of nothing if you have not first made sense of God. The study of the knowledge of God is the most important pursuit in life. Absolutely nothing is more important. We must constantly rely on Jesus Christ, our mediator, and have faithful obedience to the Word of

God. Never turn away from your source of life, your energy of life, your focus of life, which is Christ Jesus. You must have a constant reliance on Jesus Christ and faithful obedience to the Word of God. You need to put up less resistance to the painful but positive changes your spirit is leading you through. Knowing that, regardless of appearance, a divine order is always at work. You would develop the patience of a wise soul whom calmly rides out life's curveballs, knowing that these too shall pass. You would no longer be held captive by the domination of your emotions. You would be free. You will discover that the only relief from the pain you will feel lay in surrendering yourself to God, entrusting that there is a master plan at work in your life. Jeremiah 29:11–14 (NKJV) tells us,

> For I know the thoughts that I think toward you, says the Lord, thoughts of peace and not of evil, to give you a future and a hope. Then you will call upon Me and go and pray to Me, and I will listen to you. And you will seek Me and find *Me,* when you search for Me with all your heart. I will be found by you, says the Lord, and I will bring you back from your captivity; I will gather you from all the nations and from all the places where I have driven you, says the Lord, and I will bring you to the place from which I cause you to be carried away captive.

God has everything we need, but He is waiting for a greater commitment from you. He wants to give us just what we need, but He wants to add it when we come into a covenant with Him, when He knows He can trust us with it. A part of that covenant is accepting the Lord Jesus Christ as your personal Savior, which is the main part, but we need to start having a relationship with Him.

God wants covenant love, not convenient love. He wants us to commit ourselves completely, not just loving Him for what we can get out of Him. Mark 12:30 (NKJV) says, "And you shall love the Lord your God with all your heart, with all your soul, with all your mind, and with all your strength. This is the first commandment."

God also tell us in Matthew 6:33 (NKJV), "But seek first the kingdom of God and His righteousness, and all these things shall be added to you." Those who trust in Christ must reject the idea of luck or chances. God is all-knowing and sovereign over the events of our lives. God works from the inside out, sanctifying our entire being so we can live with Him forever. We must trust the Lord God for our outcome. He knows what is best. Be assured that He sees your trial, and He's with you in your test.

3

THE RHYTHM OF TIME: PAST, PRESENT, FUTURE

3

THE RHYTHM OF TIME: PAST, PRESENT, FUTURE

Story

"Once upon a time …" I start this story with those words because, on my life's journey, that's exactly what it was. Once upon a time, there were seven of us: Mama, Daddy, my two brothers, my two sisters, and me. At this juncture in my life, there is only my two sisters and I left to continue this life journey.

The Bible tells us in Ecclesiastes 3:2 (NKJV), "A time to be born and there is a time to die." My daddy went home first, and then went my younger brother, Mama, and finally my older brother. Sometimes I just sit in my easy chair, and my mind begins to go back to the good old days. I remember when we were kids. We had so much fun. During those times, your mind was never on the thought that your mother, father, and brothers would one day not be here anymore. Now that they are gone, it just doesn't seem right.

I remember the first time I experienced the death of a loved one in my family. You see, up to that point, I had never been to a funeral. It took me weeks and probably months to accept such a thing. I remember going into my parents' room just to see their chests move up and down, which meant to me they were alive. And that was such a good feeling. As my time in life has moved forward, God let me get to know His Son Jesus. Time has permitted me to accept Him as my personal Savior, establish a relationship with Him, and enjoy life knowing that we did not come to live on this earth forever.

Now when I see my family pictures and call their names, of course they will never come back to me, but one day I will go to where they are. 2 Corinthians 5:1–8 (NKJV) says,

> For we know that if our earthly house, this tent, is destroyed, we have a building from God, a house not made with hands, eternal in the heavens. For in this we groan, earnestly desiring to be clothed with our habitation which is from heaven, if indeed, having been clothed, we shall not be found naked. For we who are in this tent groan, being burdened, not because we want to be unclothed, but further clothed, that mortality may be swallowed up by life. Now He who has prepared us for this very thing is God, who also has given us the Spirit as a guarantee. So, we are always confident, knowing that while we are at home in the body we are absent from the Lord. For we walk by faith, not by sight. We are confident, yes, well pleased rather to be absent from the body and to be present with the Lord.

I discovered through my relationship with the Lord Jesus that He will calm my wondering mind concerning death. Jesus Christ will come again personally, bodily, and visibly. At His appearance, the dead in Christ will rise first, and those remaining alive will be caught up in the rapture. We must remember dying on this side means leaving one phase of life to the next, which Jesus declares would be the best thing that could ever happen to us. We get to meet "the Man" who died on Calvary for your sins and mine, "the Man" who said, "I go to prepare a place for you and if I go and prepare a place for you I will come again and receive you to Myself; that where I am there you may be also." We must be careful to believe and trust in the Jesus presented in the scriptures, the Son of God who sacrificed His life for our sins.

***

Webster defines time as "a non-spatial continuum in which events occur in apparently irreversible succession from the past through the present to the future." I would personally define time as a means of slow walking you down. Time is something you don't have control of. It will not wait on you. It just keeps ticking away. Time can be your enemy or your friend. It all depends on you. Time doesn't care if you are rich or poor, old or young, or ugly or good-looking. And it sure isn't worried about the color of your skin.

There is a time for everything and a season for every activity under heaven. There's a time to be born and a time to die. There's a time to plant and a time to uproot. There's a time to kill and a time to heal. There's a time to tear down and a time to build. There's a time to weep and a time to laugh. There's a time to mourn and a time to dance. There's a time to scatter stones and a time to gather them. There's a time to embrace and a time to refrain from embracing. There's a time to search and a time to give up. There's a time to keep and a time to throw away. There's a time to tear and a time to mend. There's a time to be silent and a time to speak. There's a time to love and a time to hate. There's a time for war and a time for peace (Ecclesiastes 3:1–8 NIV). Everything has its appointed time.

As time marches on, you learn that, apart from God, life is full of weariness and disappointment. You may be in a position in life to satisfy your every desire. You attempt to do so materially, sensually, emotionally, and intellectually, but time will slow walk you down, and you will discover that, even in the past, present, or future, life without the fear of God is empty and futile. God has given you a desire to know the future but never gives you the satisfaction of fully understanding what He does. You know that everything God does will last forever. You can't add anything to it or take anything away from it. God created us to praise Him. The overall message of Ecclesiastes 12:13 (NIV) tells us, "Fear God, and keep His commandments for this is the duty of all mankind."

Whatever happens or can happen has already happened before. God makes the same thing happen again and again. Apart from God, life has no purpose or reason. Only God can bring fulfillment, and thus our hope and trust must be in Him alone. Also in the book of Ecclesiastes, King Solomon (King David's son), the author, had more wisdom than all who were before him. King Solomon takes us on a tour of all of life and concludes that all of it is vanity. Pleasures and riches lead merely to boredom and despair. Only a relationship with the One who created us and continues to care for us will truly satisfy. Troubles and uncertainty will continue to plague us, but even during these times, we can find joy in a secure trust in our Father.

The good news is that God is the same yesterday (past), today (present), and tomorrow (future), and we must worship Him in spirit and in truth (John 4:24 NKJV). God only wants the best for you, and that is Himself. One day Jesus Christ will return, and the question is: will you be ready?

What can you do about time? Absolutely nothing! It just keeps ticking away. Again 2 Peter 3:8 (NKJV) tells us, "But, beloved, do not forget this one thing, that with the Lord one day *is* as a thousand years, and a thousand years as one day." God is eternal. God is above time. We must never think of God as being involved in the time process as we know it. It is almost impossible for us to grasp such a thought and concept, yet it is a very vital principle. We, being creatures of time and necessity, think in terms of time. God is altogether above, beyond, and outside of this time element.

Yes, to Him a thousand years are but as one day and one day as a thousand years. In other words, He does not live at all in the realm or in terms of the time process. God really is always on time. Maybe not our time, but at the right time.

We all have times in our lives when we wish we could erase the sins and failures indelibly impressed on our minds. Only as we personally put our trust in Christ as our Savior do we experience God's complete forgiveness of our sins. 1 John 1:9 (NKJV) tells us, "If we confess our sins, He is faithful and just to forgive us *our* sins and to cleanse us from all unrighteousness." Acts 13:38 (NKJV) tells us, "Therefore let it be known to you, brethren, that through this Man is preached to you the forgiveness of sins." And Acts 26:18 (NKJV) states, "To open their eyes, in order to turn them from darkness to light, and from the power of Satan to God, that they may receive forgiveness of sins and an inheritance among those who are sanctified by faith in Me."

We can't undo the past, so don't waste time trying. Instead we should devote ourselves to do God's will. This assures us that past mistakes needn't ruin our lives. Remember Christ removes our guilty past and gives us a glorious future. Romans 8:1 (AMP) tells us, "Therefore there is now no condemnation [no guilty verdict, no punishment] for those who are in Christ Jesus [who believe in Him as personal Lord and Savior."

Time

The past is like a broken hand on a clock, a clock too far away to be reached. A clock that you wish you could grab with both hands and fix, fix those small and big mistakes you have made. The mistakes you have made years ago, maybe even seconds ago—the mistakes of the past that cannot be changed.

The present is the time right now, right this second; the tiny little thoughts that are going through your mind, as you read this or as I read this to you. The present time is the time that decides the future of life and the future of this world.

The future is the time unknown, only thought about. The time that is like a mirror, a reflection of the present and past times. A time that is only seen by God, a time that is soon to be seen.

R.A.S

God's Love

God's love is everlasting.
It is the highest form of love you can gain.
Once you have Him in your life, you can never be the same.
God's love is like a river, flowing through your soul,
Sins wash away as clean as a slate when you pray to the
Lord for His almighty forgiveness.
God's Love enables you to get up in the
morning and go to bed at night.
Though one day you will be dead to the world,
You still have to remember that if you have God's Love,
You can go on to a better place, a heavenly place,
A place where God's Love never dies away.
R.A.S.

Perfect Love

Everyone longs to give themselves completely to someone. To have a deep soul relationship with another, to be loved thoroughly and exclusively. But God to the Christian says, "No, not until you're satisfied and fulfilled, and content with living, loved by Me alone, and giving yourself totally and unreservedly to Me to have an intensely personal and unique relationship with Me alone. I love you My child, and until you discover that only in Me is your satisfaction to be found, you will not be capable of the perfect human relationship that I have planned for you. You will never be united with another until you are united with Me exclusive of anyone or anything else, exclusive of any other desires or longings. I want you stop planning, stop wishing, and allow Me to bring it to you. You must keep watching Me, expecting the greatest things. Keep learning and listening to the things I tell you. *You must wait.*

"Don't be anxious and don't worry. Don't look at things you think you want. Just keep looking off and away up to Me, or you'll miss what I have to show you.

"And then, when you're ready, I'll surprise you with a love far more wonderful than any you would ever dream of. You see, until you are ready and until the one I have for you is ready, I am working this minute to have both of you ready at the same time, and until you are both satisfied exclusively with Me. This is perfect love.

—Unknown Author

Since Christ Jesus gives us loyal love, why can't we give Him loyal faith? Why can't we just believe what He says when He says it? Romans 8:38–39 (NKJV) tells us, "For I am persuaded that neither death nor life, nor angels nor principalities nor powers, nor things present nor things to come, nor height nor depth, nor any other created thing, shall be able to separate us from the love of God which is in Christ Jesus our Lord." Now that's loyalty.

4

THE RHYTHM OF YOUR SOUL: YOU DON'T OWN IT

4

THE RHYTHM OF YOUR SOUL: YOU DON'T OWN IT

Story

I have a confession. This story is about a period in my life I have never discussed with anyone other than the Lord Jesus and myself. I remember my first marriage at the age of nineteen. He and I were both just getting out of high school, but we were so much in love with each other. I became pregnant right after high school, and we decided to get married. Back then, we couldn't imagine not being together for the rest of our lives. But as time progressed, we started growing apart. I began to attend church more, and every now and then, he would accompany me.

Unfortunately, he started beginning to love the streets and his friends more than our baby and me. He began testing the waters with drugs and eventually became hooked. He tried several times going through drug rehabilitation, but it was short-lived because he would not let go of the streets and addicted friends. He was addicted to drugs, and I was addicted to him. But I drew so tired of being stressed to the limit. Being a mother and father at the same time was more than I could bear. And then I became pregnant with our third child. I didn't share my pregnancy with anyone. Unfortunately, it was at a time in my life and marriage that the thought of bringing another baby in the world with a marriage to a drug-addicted husband who struggled being a good father and did not appreciate having a good wife at his side just wasn't sitting right with me anymore.

Though I was in church and getting to know God, my marriage had pretty much reached rock bottom. I didn't or wouldn't believe that God could save my marriage and change my husband's heart and mind. I just knew I couldn't have another baby by this man. I wasn't going to do it!

Even though I felt like there was something trying to reach me to not abort this fetus I was carrying inside of me, as days rolled by, I was too busy concentrating on my bad marriage and not praying to God to help me in my situation. I only had a few more weeks left to make my final decision to abort this fetus. I made myself feel better by saying it was a fetus and not a soul.

One night, I just felt like ending what was causing all this unrest inside of me. It was my husband, and I wanted to hurt him as he had hurt me over and over again, time after time. I just wanted to get rid of him for causing all this calamity and pain in my life, but I was not raised to do such a thing. I was not thinking that aborting this baby was the same thing, but at that time, I didn't look at a fetus as a real person with a soul carrying the very breath of God.

The night before it was time to report to the clinic, I did not sleep a wink. I felt like what was inside of me was trying to contact my inner self, somewhat begging to be left alone, but me, myself, and I wasn't having it. I wanted this out of me and to be free of going another nine months being pregnant and living with a drug-driven husband.

The day of the procedure, again what was inside of me kept nudging at me, but I refused to listen. So the abortion was performed, and that night I began to feel regret and disappointment in myself. Why didn't I listen to my baby begging to be left alone and thereby allowing him or her to come to full term and get a chance to live? Why would I destroy what God was knitting in my womb? (Psalm 139:13–16).

Why? Because I turned a deaf ear to any emotion or concern. I was on a mission and determined to fulfill that undertaking. Of course, at this juncture in my life, my relationship with the Lord is stronger, and my mind-set is more stable for the better of doing right in the sight of God. When we realize on this life journey that we will answer to a higher power, we will listen more and obey more.

To me, telling this story is somewhat of a confession and a relief of something that has been lying dormant inside of me for years upon years. I know God has forgiven me because I have truly asked for forgiveness. His Word in Ephesians 1:7 (NKJV) states, "In Him we have redemption through His Blood, the forgiveness of sins, according to the riches of His Grace."

***

Below is a sonogram of my grandchild in my daughter's womb. I was so mesmerized looking at this small human being inside of another person growing day by day.

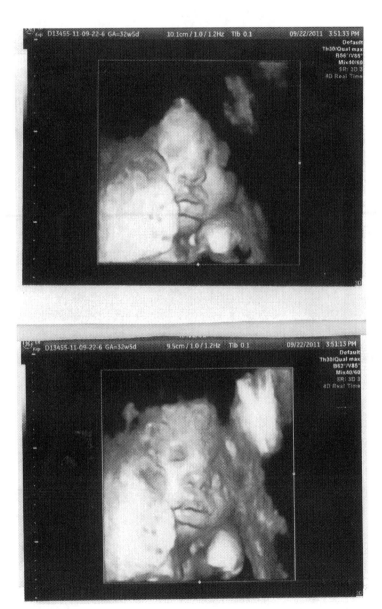

Now who can do such a thing as this, except God? All of Psalm 139, which is authored by King David, talks about God's perfect knowledge of man. The idea is that the life of a person and the structure and meaning of that individual's life are all established from the beginning by God. We are indeed fearfully and wonderfully made. Life can be strong as well as weak.

Once we take our first breath in the world and are allowed to grow up to make decisions and choices in life, that's when we discover that some of the choices we make can make us or break us. We should make sure one of the most important choices we can make is to accept Christ as our personal Saviour. The one who has given you the gift of life should be most appreciated out of anything else in this world. We need to learn to be more grateful to God and count it a pleasure to have experienced life on this earth.

Your soul is the spiritual principle embodied in human beings. God gave us a will, a mind to reason and to think with, and a heart filled with passion. Contrary to your thinking or believing, let's get one thing straight. Your soul does not belong to you. Your soul is a gift from God. The Lord gave it, and He sure can take it away. And He will once this thing we call death overtakes us. That soul that God breathed into our nostrils will one day return to the provider. If you think about it, God is so awesome. His infinite wisdom can hold the souls of all living creatures, and with one inhale, He can pull it all back. But instead He chooses to allow us to use it finitely. We don't realize how significant it is that we carry the very breath of God inside us. In Genesis 2:7 (NKJV), Moses wrote, "And the Lord God formed man of the dust of the ground, and breathed into his nostrils the breath of life and man became a living being."

This breath may be Moses's way of describing the infusion of the human spirit with its moral, intellectual, relational, and spiritual capacities. God showed tender care and intimate concern in the way He shaped man. It is good to be able to enjoy the pleasant light of day. Be grateful for every year you live. Our bodies will return to the dust of the earth, and the breath of life will go back to God, who gave it to us. Your soul is God's breath. The Holy Spirit keeps you in check, always remembering what His true mission is, to refine you, to strengthen you, to purify you, and to keep you worthy.

Everywhere you see adversity, the soul sees the opportunity for our healing, expansion, and enlightenment. Your dilemmas, your difficulties, your predicaments, and how you face and handle them define who you are, why you're here, what you're trying to do, and what you're trying to achieve through earth-plane existence. Those things neither purify nor strengthen you. Nor do they refine you. But being hammered in fire does. You mistakenly believe that the pursuit of happiness, comfort, ease, security, and status are the goal of life, but your soul has another agenda altogether. It cares nothing for the personality's suffering, only that there be the refinement, the strengthening, and the purification so the personality is rendered worthy to serve your soul's purpose.

You should never place your heart and soul in the hands of another. Those two belong to God, who is your soul provider. Know that, since He is the provider of the soul, then He is able to heal the soul when it needs it. God tells us in Matthew 10:28 (NKJV), "And do not fear those who kill the body but cannot kill the soul. But rather fear Him who is able to destroy both soul and body in hell."

God also tells us in Deuteronomy 6:5 (NKJV), "You shall love the Lord your God with all your heart, with all your soul, and with all your strength." If we "all" would just obey and believe, just think how peaceful our lives and our world would be, which is just the way God planned for it to be.

I would like to conclude this book with the following "Commitment as a Christian," written by a young African pastor (name unknown). This should be your pledge for life. Please sign it, date it, and keep it.

I _____ Date _____
(your name)

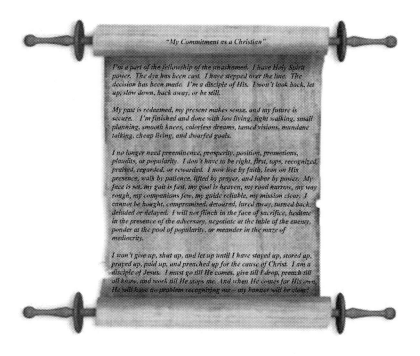

"My Commitment as a Christian"

I'm a part of the fellowship of the unashamed. I have Holy Spirit power. The die has been cast. I have stepped over the line. The decision has been made. I'm a disciple of His. I won't look back, let up, slow down, back away, or be still.

My past is redeemed, my present makes sense, and my future is secure. I'm finished and done with low living, sight walking, small planning, smooth knees, colorless dreams, tamed visions, mundane talking, cheap living, and dwarfed goals.

I no longer need preeminence, prosperity, position, promotions, plaudits, or popularity. I don't have to be right, first, tops, recognized, praised, regarded, or rewarded. I now live by faith, lean on His presence, walk by patience, lifted by prayer, and labor by power. My face is set, my gait is fast, my goal is heaven, my road narrow, my way rough, my companions few, my guide reliable, my mission clear. I cannot be bought, compromised, detoured, lured away, turned back, deluded or delayed. I will not flinch in the face of sacrifice, hesitate in the presence of the adversary, negotiate at the table of the enemy, ponder at the pool of popularity, or meander in the maze of mediocrity.

I won't give up, shut up, and let up until I have stayed up, stored up, prayed up, paid up, and preached up for the cause of Christ. I am a disciple of Jesus. I must go till He comes, give till I drop, preach till all know, and work till He stops me. And when He comes for His own, He will have no problem recognizing me — my banner will be clear.

God's peace is experienced through your sustained trust and belief in Him and a continual love for the Word of God that is demonstrated by living in wholehearted obedience and keeping your life, your time, and your soul in divine rhythm.

"And the beat goes on" will stop one day. Will you be ready?

Printed in the United States
By Bookmasters